BLS WORKING PAPERS

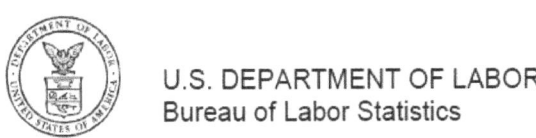

U.S. DEPARTMENT OF LABOR
Bureau of Labor Statistics

OFFICE OF PRICES AND LIVING
CONDITIONS

The Behavior of Intrafirm Trade Prices in
U.S. International Price Data

Kimberly A. Clausing, Reed College

Working Paper 333
January 2001

The views expressed are those of the author and do not necessarily reflect the policies of the U.S. Bureau of Labor Statistics or the views of other staff members.   This paper was part of the U.S. Bureau of Labor Statistics Conference on *Issues in Measuring Price Change and Consumption* in Washington, DC, June 2000.

The Behavior of Intrafirm Trade Prices in U.S. International Price Data

June 2000

Kimberly A. Clausing
Asst. Professor of Economics
Reed College
3203 SE Woodstock Blvd.
Portland, OR 97202-8199
U.S.A.
(503) 771-1112, x7388
email: clausing@reed.edu

Abstract: This paper analyzes data from the Bureau of Labor Statistics on international prices between 1997 and 1999 in order to investigate the pricing patterns of intrafirm trade. The results indicate several important ways in which intrafirm trade prices differ from non-intrafirm prices. First, intrafirm trade prices appear to be influenced by the tax-minimization strategies of multinational firms. There is a strong and statistically significant relationship between countries' tax rates and the prices of intrafirm imports and exports exchanged with those countries. Second, intrafirm trade prices are typically more correlated with exchange rate variables. Third, price changes for intrafirm trade products are less frequent. Still, the overall price patterns for intrafirm trade are quite similar to those for non-intrafirm trade. The average magnitudes of price changes are comparable, and the patterns of price changes over time are also similar.

I. Introduction

Since 1971, the Bureau of Labor Statistics (BLS) has been charged with the collection of international price data, which is used to compile import and export price indexes. To collect this data, BLS economists survey firms to determine the prices of given imported and exported goods, and how these prices change over time. In contrast to the collection of producer prices, the collection of international prices includes price information from substantial amounts of intrafirm transactions, or transactions between different affiliates of the same multinational firm. If the data is to be representative of the overall prices of U.S. international transactions, the inclusion of intrafirm trade is absolutely necessary; intrafirm trade accounts for a large share -- approximately 40% -- of all U.S. international trade. Still, the inclusion of intrafirm trade raises some important concerns.

To the extent that intrafirm trade behaves differently from arms-length trade, the inclusion of intrafirm trade is likely to affect intrafirm trade indexes. Previous research has often emphasized ways in which intrafirm trade may differ from arms-length trade. For example, intrafirm trade may be influenced by the tax minimization strategies of multinational firms, as demonstrated by Clausing (1998) and others. Intrafirm trade may respond differently to exchange rate changes, as hypothesized by Rangan and Lawrence (1999). In addition, intrafirm trade may differ from arms-length trade in other respects as well. Some have hypothesized that intrafirm trade is more likely to be based on cost factors than on market-based demand considerations. Further, to the extent that multinational firms are different from other firms, one might expect that their trade patterns would also differ.

This paper utilizes data from the BLS on international prices in 1997, 1998, and 1999 to undertake an empirical investigation of the pricing patterns of intrafirm trade. There are two basic aims. First, the paper considers how BLS price indexes are influenced by the inclusion of intrafirm trade. Second, the paper investigates more generally the pricing behavior of intrafirm trade, in order to achieve an improved understanding of how intrafirm trade may differ from trade conducted at arms-length.

Results indicate that intrafirm trade prices do differ from arms-length trade prices in several important ways: these prices are more sensitive to tax variables, these prices are typically more sensitive to exchange rate variables, and price changes for intrafirm trade products are less frequent. That said, the overall pattern of price changes for intrafirm trade is quite similar to the pattern for arms-length trade. Price changes are typically of similar magnitudes, and follow similar paths over time. Hence it appears that the inclusion of intrafirm trade in international price indexes is unlikely to affect overall inferences based on U.S. international price data. This is reassuring since the inclusion of intrafirm trade in such indexes is warranted due to its quantitative importance in U.S. international trade.

II. Background

The Behavior of Intrafirm Trade

Before addressing the BLS methodology of collecting international price information, it is useful to first discuss how intrafirm trade is likely to differ from trade conducted at arms-length. In particular, what are the theoretical reasons to suspect that intrafirm trade might behave differently empirically?

3

In a previous paper (Clausing (1998)), I have demonstrated that U.S. intrafirm trade flows appear to be affected by the tax minimization strategies of multinational firms. In particular, the evidence suggests that the United States has less favorable intrafirm trade balances with low tax countries. This result is anticipated if multinational firms are manipulating transfer prices in order to shift income to low tax countries. For example, there would be an incentive to underprice U.S. intrafirm exports to low tax countries and overprice U.S. intrafirm imports from such countries, following the opposite strategy with respect to transactions with high-tax countries.

Following Horst (1971) and Kant (1995), one can produce a simple model that generates the prediction that intrafirm trade prices will be affected by the tax minimization strategies of multinational firms. Consider a multinational firm with some degree of market power that is operating in two countries. It produces and sells in each country, and also exports part of its output from the home country (1) to the affiliate abroad (2).[1] For now, assume that the affiliate is fully owned.[2]

Profit functions for operations in the two countries are given by the following equations:

$$\pi_1 = R_1(s_1) - C_1(s_1 + m) + pm \qquad (1)$$

$$\pi_2 = R_2(s_2) - C_2(s_2 - m) - pm \qquad (2)$$

π_1 is profit in the home country, which depends on revenues R_1 that are a function of sales, s_1, and costs C_1 that are a function of production. Production includes both those

---

[1] It is straightforward to extend this model to consider trade that originates in the affiliate country. One can also consider this trade to be in intermediate products without affecting the basic insights developed here.
[2] The implications of relaxing this assumption are considered in Kant (1995) and briefly discussed below.

goods sold at home, and those sent to the affiliate abroad, m. The output that is exported

to the affiliates abroad is given the transfer price p.

Consider the case where tax rates at home are greater than tax rates abroad $(t_1 > t_2)$

and deferral is allowed. Let f represent the fraction of profits that are repatriated. The

effective tax rate on income earned in the affiliate country is then:

$$t_2^e = t_2 + (t_1 - t_2) f \tag{3}$$

The net profit function for the firm's global operations is:

$$\pi = (1-t_1) \pi_1 + (1-t_2^e) \pi_2 \tag{4}$$

To illustrate how the firm may choose a transfer price in order to maximize these net

profits, consider the derivative of (4) with respect to the transfer price, p.

$$\pi_p = (1-t_1) m - (1-t_2^e) m \tag{5}$$

Substituting for t_2^e using (3) and rearranging,

$$\pi_p = -(t_1-t_2) (1-f) m \tag{6}$$

So, if $t_1 > t_2$, the above expression is negative, and the firm's net profits decrease with the

transfer price. Thus, firms have an incentive to underprice goods sold to low tax

countries in order to shift profits to low tax locations. Similarly, one can show that firms

have an incentive to overprice goods sold to high tax affiliates when $t_2 > t_1$.[3] [4]

---

[3]Note that these models implicitly assume that there is only one transfer price p; that is, firms keep just one set of books. Firms in reality may keep more than one set of books, using one set of prices to minimize tax liabilities and other sets of prices for other purposes such as determining the relative performance of affiliates.

[4] As Kant (1990) reminds us, though, two considerations may interfere with this motivation. First of all, firms may be subject to penalties if their manipulation of transfer prices is too flagrant. If the probability of receiving a penalty increases as the transfer price is further from the arms-length price, firms will likely choose a transfer price that balances the gain from profit shifting with the possibility of a penalty. This consideration alters the degree of transfer price manipulation, but would not alter the desired direction of underpricing or overpricing. Second, affiliates may not be wholly owned. This creates a second profit

This model suggests one dimension in which intrafirm trade may behave differently from arms-length trade.[5] Putting aside tax considerations, there is no reason to assume that intrafirm trade will be similar in all other respects, given the literature on multinational enterprises, which has emphasized several special characteristics of these firms. For instance, the *OLI paradigm* (described in more detail in Caves (1996)) stresses that multinational firms arise due to ownership, location, and internalization advantages. These advantages make it optimal to undertake activity within one multinational firm rather than among separate, national firms. Depending on one's perspective, such advantages may enable multinational firms to respond more quickly or with greater magnitudes to changes in economic variables. For instance, Rangan and Lawrence (1999, p.14-15) argue that :

> Multinationals with foreign facilities are likely to have an advantage. Even the routine operation of those facilities generates a set of business relationships, a continually replenished stock of information about actual prices, and detailed knowledge about the existence, location, and precise needs and capabilities of buyers and suppliers in that region. Hence, the multinational is conferred with privileged access to valuable information and connections...[6]

---

shifting incentive, as firms may choose to overprice shipments to affiliates to transfer profits to sources that are wholly owned and away from partially owned sources. While this consideration may influence the desired direction of transfer price changes, it also assumes that firms are free to manipulate transfer prices without the need to be responsive to the profits of their minority interests.

[5] However, it is important to note that such models have direct implications about the *price* of intrafirm trade transactions, but have less direct implications about the volumes of intrafirm trade. For instance, such models may lead one to expect that intrafirm exports to low tax countries would be under-priced. However, this need not imply lower *volumes* of intrafirm trade, since quantities of such trade may increase at the same time that prices are lower. In fact, this is what one would expect. Since intrafirm trade can generate tax savings, it is optimal for firms to increase the volume of such trade relative to its level in the absence of such considerations. See Eden (1998, p.298). In addition, a low tax country may attract more foreign direct investment in general, and this in turn would act to increase volumes of intrafirm trade with such a country in both directions.

[6] For arguments about the greater responsiveness of multinational firms, see also Knetter (1993), Lipsey and Kravis (1986), and Little (1986).

Or, it is possible that the large size of multinational enterprises would generate more ponderous decision making processes, and inhibit the firms' responsiveness to changes in economic conditions. As multinationals invest in different countries, they may become increasingly integrated with the local economy, and less likely to respond to changes in economic variables rapidly.[7] Finally, some have argued that there is little reason one would expect any difference between the behavior of intrafirm trade and trade conducted at arms-length.[8] [9]

In addition, authors have argued that intrafirm trade prices are more likely to be based on cost considerations than on market value, and that intrafirm trade prices are likely to change less frequently and/or more dramatically. (See, e.g., Alterman (1997b), p.16.) One might also suspect that intrafirm trade would be different in other respects. For example, it may be the case that intrafirm trade would be possible in situations of imperfect information where arms-length markets fail. For instance, the *internalization* advantages that are part of the OLI framework emphasize the difficulties associated with licensing proprietary information. In an environment of imperfect information, it might be easier to transact some products within the firm than at arms-length. In addition, the

---

[7] For similar arguments, see Goldsbrough (1981), Little (1986), and Encarnation (1992).
[8] See, for example, Caves (1996, p.33).
[9] Rangan and Lawrence (1999) have undertaken work examining whether intrafirm trade responds differently to exchange rate changes. They find that the trade of U.S. multinational firms is indeed sensitive to exchange rate changes, especially if one adjusts for the industry composition of U.S. multinational firms and if one considers how sourcing decisions respond to exchange rate changes. They also hypothesize that intrafirm trade may respond more quickly to exchange rate changes than does arms-length trade due to the informational advantages associated with the superior international networks of multinational firms. Their empirical work finds support for this view.

product composition of intrafirm trade is likely to be different from arms-length trade, including more intermediate goods and fewer final products.[10]

In summary, intrafirm trade may behave differently for at least three reasons. First, it may be more sensitive to tax influences. Second, it may be more or less responsive to changes in economic variables such as exchange rates. Third, the composition of intrafirm trade could differ from that of conventional trade in ways that would affect its behavior.

Intrafirm Trade and BLS Methodology

The International Price Program (IPP) of the BLS is charged with producing data on the prices of U.S. international trade. The IPP collects monthly information on prices for approximately 22,000 items, and uses this information to generate import and export price indexes. The program publishes over 700 detailed and aggregate trade price indexes. These indexes are used for a variety of purposes, including deflating trade volume statistics, measuring inflation, performing elasticity studies, deriving terms of trade indexes and real exchange rates, and forming trade contracts.

In contrast to the trade price indexes, the producer price index (PPI) normally does not include goods that are being sold from one part of a firm to another. As Alterman (1997a) explains, "Under the definition of a *net* output index, these so-called intra-company transfers are considered out-of-scope of the PPI when the different branches of the same company are considered to be in the same industry." However, the

---

[10] In a recent paper (Clausing, 2000), I have demonstrated that the empirical behavior of intrafirm trade in a gravity equation model differs substantially from that of arms-length trade. First, the gravity model, long the most empirically successful model of international trade flows, has far less explanatory power with respect to intrafirm trade than with respect to arms-length trade. Second, most of the individual coefficients in the model are substantially different with respect to the two types of trade.

8

export and import price indexes are meant to represent the universe of goods that are traded, and hence include substantial amounts of intrafirm trade transactions. Given the large share of U.S. international trade that is conducted within the firm (approximately 40%), the inclusion of intrafirm trade in these price indexes is surely necessary.

Still, prior to 1998, the IPP only included intrafirm transactions that were deemed to be "market-based" or "market-influenced". This policy changed in February 1998, however, when the IPP began including all intrafirm transactions. In mid-1998, the IPP also began collecting information on the pricing method used for intrafirm transactions. Firms are asked whether they use market-based pricing, cost-based pricing, or "other, non-market based" pricing, but all types of intrafirm trade prices are used.

This methodology raises several important sets of questions. First, what influence does the inclusion of intrafirm trade have on U.S. import and export price indexes? While it is likely appropriate to include intrafirm trade in trade price indexes, are there issues that one should be aware of in terms of how such indexes are affected by intrafirm trade? Second, how useful is the distinction between "market-based" intrafirm trade and other types? Do the prices of these types of trade behave differently? Is it appropriate to include all types of intrafirm trade in trade price indexes?

III. Data Analysis

This paper will undertake an empirical analysis of BLS data on export and import prices with the aim of addressing how the inclusion of intrafirm trade is affecting trade price indexes, as well as the aim of understanding how intrafirm trade behaves more generally. The following questions will be central to this analysis.

- Is there evidence of tax-motivated transfer pricing for intrafirm trade? In particular, is there evidence that the prices of intrafirm trade goods are sensitive to the tax rates of the countries with whom the good is traded?

- Does intrafirm trade appear to be more or less sensitive to exchange rate changes, compared to arms-length trade?

- More generally, does the pattern of price changes differ for intrafirm trade? Do price changes differ in size? Are price changes more or less frequent?

- Does one find different patterns for market-based intrafirm trade compared with other types of intrafirm trade?

The analysis employs monthly data on trade prices over three years: 1997, 1998, and 1999. Table 1 describes some of the key features of this data. There are over 425,000 observations of monthly prices. 33% of these observations are for exports, and 38% of observations are intrafirm trade. A wide variety of countries are included. However, for the analysis that includes tax or exchange rate variables, data limitations restrict the data set to observations from 54 countries;[11] this restricted data set is the data set described in Table 1.

Table 2 shows the first comparisons of intrafirm and non-intrafirm trade prices: this table considers the average price changes for observations in the entire sample. For intrafirm trade, the average year over year change in price of a good is -.013, or a fall in price of 1.3%. This is quite similar to the average change in price for the sample of non-intrafirm goods, where the average fall in price is 1.1%. Considering instead the absolute value of the change in price allows one to examine the average magnitudes of price changes. Again, intrafirm trade is almost indistinguishable from non-intrafirm trade. Goods traded intrafirm see an average year over year price change of 7.4%, compared with an average price change of 7.5% for non-intrafirm trade. Somewhat larger differences in price patterns stand out if we consider the frequency of monthly price changes. For the sample of intrafirm goods, 40.8% of observations experience a monthly price change. For non-intrafirm goods, price changes are more frequent; 45.1% of observations indicate monthly price changes. When one divides the sample into exports and imports, slightly larger differences are observed for the price change variables, and intrafirm trade continues to exhibit less frequent monthly price changes.

The similarity in price patterns for intrafirm and non-intrafirm trade is also demonstrated graphically in figures 1 and 2. Figure 1 shows the average monthly price changes for all of the observations in the sample over the period January 1997 to December 1999. Figure 1a shows both exports and imports, while figures 1b and 1c show exports and imports separately. Several features of the data are of interest. First, the price changes exhibit noticeable patterns over time. Second, price trends for intrafirm and non-intrafirm trade are *very* similar, particularly for imports, but also for exports. When these average trade price changes are used to create an index in Figure 2, the overall similarities continue to stand out. The import indexes are quite similar, in particular. Non-intrafirm export price changes appear to be slightly more volatile in the first part of the sample, and appear to be greater during the last seven months of the sample.

Table 3 shows the same information as Table 2, broken down by 2-digit SITC industry. The sample-wide averages obscure a substantial amount of industry variation in

---

[11] In particular, there is data on tax information from the Bureau of Economic Analysis for this set of countries; these are also the countries for which I have collected exchange rate data.

price patterns. While it is sometimes the case that price changes are similar for intrafirm and non-intrafirm trade, this is not the case for all industries.[12]

Table 4 shows the share of observations that are intrafirm trade, by two-digit SITC industry. For the entire sample, 38% of observations are intrafirm trade. However, this figure masks important differences across industries. For example, for SITC industry #54, or medicinal and pharmaceutical products, 65% of observations are intrafirm trade, while 18% of the observations from the fruit and vegetable industry (SITC #05) are intrafirm trade. Table 4 also shows the breakdown of observations by different types of intrafirm trade: market-based, cost-based, "other", and not classified. The later category accounts for the majority of the intrafirm observations as this data was only collected for items initiated into the BLS survey after mid-1998. Still, for those intrafirm goods that are classified, one notices substantial differences in the percentage of intrafirm trade that is market-based across industries.[13]

Table 5 also shows the same information as Table 2, but now breaks the data down by type of trade to examine more carefully the differences in price behavior between different types of intrafirm trade. We again find intrafirm price patterns that are similar to non-intrafirm patterns. The average price change hovers just over zero for market and cost-based intrafirm trade and near −1% for non-classified intrafirm trade and non-intrafirm trade. The exception is intrafirm trade that is classified as something other than market or cost based; this trade experiences larger price declines. In addition, these "other" observations also experience larger average absolute changes in prices (13.3%)

---

[12] Table 3 includes only those industries with more than 100 observations for all of the variables. Complete tables of all industries are available upon request. However, one should be particularly wary of making

than the other categories of trade, where average price changes are between 7.3% and 8.6% for the entire sample.[14]

Larger differences stand out if one considers the frequency of price changes. Intrafirm prices change less frequently, particularly when prices are cost-based or something other than market or cost-based. 37% of cost-based observations indicate monthly changes in price; 29% of "other" observations do. And even market based intrafirm trade observations experience fewer price changes (41% of observations) than non-intrafirm observations (45%).

Regression Analysis

After the above consideration of the data on intrafirm price changes, it appears that (overall) intrafirm trade price behavior is not substantially different from non-intrafirm trade. In particular, price changes tend to be of similar magnitudes, and to follow similar paths over time, even though prices do change somewhat less frequently for intrafirm trade. However, we have not yet addressed the more subtle questions raised above. For instance, even though the average price patterns may be similar, it is possible that intrafirm trade reacts differently to changes in exchange rates or to tax influences.

In the following analysis, I have merged the BLS data on monthly product prices together with data on monthly exchange rates, and data on tax rates across countries. The monthly exchange rate data have been used to derive a monthly exchange rate index for each country in order to see how exchange rates have influenced prices over this time

---

inferences regarding the differences in price patterns for the industries with few observations.

[13] Industries with fewer than 300 (total) monthly observations are indicated with an asterix.

[14] Dividing the sample into exports and imports, one observes similar price changes for intrafirm and non-intrafirm trade, the exception again being the "other" category. Again, average absolute changes in prices

period.[15] In addition, I have included data on the effective tax rate of the

destination/origin countries gathered from the Bureau of Economic Analysis surveys on

U.S. direct investment abroad; this tax variable is generated using data from 1997 and

varies only across countries, not over time. The effective tax rate is calculated as the

foreign income taxes paid by U.S. affiliates in a given country divided to by their pre-tax

net income.[16] [17]

Table 6 estimates regressions explaining the prices of products in the sample.

Separate regressions are estimated for intrafirm trade and non-intrafirm trade, and for

exports and imports.

$$\ln(\text{Price}_{it}) = \alpha + \beta_1 \ln(\text{Exchange Rate Index}_{it}) + \beta_2 \ln(1\text{-Effective Tax Rate}_{it}) + \beta_3$$
$$\text{Inpute}_{it} + \beta_4 \text{Link}_{it} + \beta_5 \text{NoDollar}_{it} + \beta_z \text{Industry Dummies} + \upsilon_{it}$$

All variables except dummy variables are in natural logs; i indicates individual

products and t indicates months. Dummy variables are used for goods where the price

---

are near 7% for most categories, with the exceptions of market and cost based intrafirm exports and "other" intrafirm imports, which experience larger absolute price changes.

[15] I use monthly exchange rate data from the University of British Columbia web site http://pacific.commerce.ubc.ca/xr/data.html. This page and the FX database software are © 1998-99 by Prof. Werner Antweiler, University of British Columbia, Vancouver, Canada. Similar data on exchange rates are also available from several other sources.

[16] While using marginal tax rates is a theoretically superior alternative, using marginal tax rates in practice is very difficult. First, it is harder to get comparable data for this sample of 54 countries. Second, the published marginal tax rates are an imperfect proxy for the actual tax rates firms face since such rates do not account for the many subtleties (tax holidays, ad hoc arrangements, special allowances, etc.) that determine the true tax treatment of firms. In fact, several studies have shown that effective tax rates are commonly quite different from statutory rates, often due to the provision of special tax incentives. See, e.g., Buijink, et al, (1999).

[17] I have checked the results of this analysis using two alternative tax variables. The first was an average effective tax rate for the years 1993-1997, again calculated using BEA data. This average tax variable should correct for any anomalies of 1997 that could be affecting the results. Second, I used a average effective tax variable calculated by Altshuler et al. (1998) using data from U.S. corporate income tax (5471) forms for 1992. In both cases, the results are quite similar using the alternative variables. This is perhaps not surprising given the high correlation between these alternative variables (.93 and .79, respectively) and the variable used here.

has been inputed, for goods where a "link price" has been estimated[18], and for goods

where the price is not expressed in dollars. In addition, dummy variables are included for

SITC 2-digit industries. Expectations regarding the coefficients are as follows.

	Expected Sign	Justification
β_1	-	As the dollar is stronger, export and import prices should both be lower.
β_2	IF<NIF for exports; IF>NIF for imports	Prices of intrafirm exports should be lower than non-intrafirm exports for low-tax countries (when (1-Effective Tax Rate) is high). Prices of intrafirm imports should be higher than non-intrafirm imports for low-tax countries.
β_3	?	Inputed prices may be higher or lower than normal.
β_4	+ ?	When link prices are estimated, prices may be higher or lower than normal. An improvement in quality would generally raise prices.[19]
β_5	?	When prices are not quoted in dollars, prices may be higher or lower than usual.
β_z	+ or -	Prices are likely to vary by industry.

Results are in Table 6. For both exports and imports, intrafirm trade appears to be

more sensitive to variations in exchange rates. A dollar index that is one percent stronger

is associated with 1.5 percent lower intrafirm export prices and .73 percent lower

intrafirm import prices; for non-intrafirm trade, export prices are .56 percent lower and

import prices are .4 percent lower. Lower prices are consistently associated with

countries with low effective tax rates. (I have no good explanation for this finding.) For

exports, however, this association is larger (by a factor of 6) for intrafirm exports than for

---

[18] Link prices are used by the BLS in the place of reported prices when survey items have changed. The aim is to calculate a price at which the old item would have traded in the new time period. In the analysis here, I use the non-link prices rather than the link prices, noting that the presence of link prices may lead to

non-intrafirm exports. This would be expected if multinational firms are more likely to underprice goods sold to low tax countries in order to shift profit away from such locations. For imports, the negative association is much larger for non-intrafirm goods than for intrafirm goods. This could also support tax minimization incentives since multinational firms would prefer higher prices on intrafirm goods purchased *from* low tax countries.

In terms of other variables, results indicate that goods with inputed prices are likely to have higher prices in the three cases where this variable is statistically significant. Goods where a link price is available are likely to have higher prices. Finally, goods that are not priced in dollars are also likely to have higher prices. All specifications include industry dummies for industries at the SITC 2-digit level of aggregation. These dummies are typically highly statistically significant, and they also much improve the explanatory power of the regression as a whole.[20]

Table 7 shows regressions similar to those in Table 6, but now intrafirm trade is estimated together with non-intrafirm trade. This approach leads to similar overall conclusions but allows a clearer investigation of how intrafirm trade is different form non-intrafirm trade. A dummy variable is included to indicate when trade is intrafirm. In

---

expected changes in the non-link prices. For example, if the quality of the good has improved, using the normal price rather than a link price would lead to a higher observed price.

[19] However, there are many other reasons for a link price including unit changes, discounts, or others.

[20] Regressions is tables 6,7, and 8 all include industry dummies for industries at the SITC 2-digit level of aggregation. It is also useful to consider industry dummies at an even more disaggregate level, such as 4 digit. This enables a comparison of prices, controlling for the (more finely classified) industry of the product. One can then ask whether intrafirm trade within such industries behaves differently. With this data, however, one runs into computer memory problems with such a large regression matrix and so many observations. Therefore, I limited the analysis to one month of data at a time. Running the same baseline regressions as reported in the text, I typically found quite similar results with the more disaggregate industry dummy variables. This may ameliorate concerns that it is the industry composition of intrafirm trade, rather than the intrafirm nature of such trade, that is driving these results.

addition, interaction terms are included to indicate whether, when trade is intrafirm, its responsiveness to exchange rates or tax rates differs substantially. The equation estimated is:

$$\ln(\text{Price}_{it}) = \alpha + \beta_1 \text{ Intrafirm Dummy}_{it} + \beta_2 \ln(\text{Exchange Rate Index}_{it}) + \beta_3 \ln(1-\text{Effective Tax Rate}_{it}) + \beta_4 \ln(\text{Exchange Rate Index}_{it})*\text{Intrafirm Dummy}_{it} + \beta_5 \ln(1-\text{Effective Tax Rate}_{it})*\text{Intrafirm Dummy}_{it} + \beta_6 \text{ Input}e_{it} + \beta_7 \text{ Link}_{it} + \beta_8 \text{ NoDollar}_{it} + \beta_z \text{ Industry Dummies} + \upsilon_{it}$$

The coefficient β_4 is expected to be negative if intrafirm trade is more responsive to exchange rates, and positive if intrafirm trade is less responsive to exchange rates. If tax-motivated transfer pricing is important, the coefficient β_5 is expected to be negative for exports and positive for imports. In particular, intrafirm exports to low-tax countries should have lower prices as multinational firms attempt to shift profits to such locations whereas intrafirm imports from such low-tax countries should have higher prices.

Turning to the results, the coefficient on the intrafirm dummy variable indicates that intrafirm prices are typically larger, controlling for the other variables in the regression. All trade is associated with the exchange rate index variable in the hypothesized direction: when the dollar is one percent more appreciated, this is associated with export prices .62 % lower and import prices .42% lower. Intrafirm trade is even more strongly associated with the exchange rate variable, particularly intrafirm exports. A dollar exchange rate index that is 1% more appreciated is associated with a further 1% reduction in intrafirm export prices and a further .34% reduction in intrafirm import prices.

Lower prices again tend to be associated with countries with low effective tax rates. However, for trade that is intrafirm, export prices are lower, while import prices are higher. Both of these tax interaction terms are highly statistically significant. The estimates indicate that a tax rate one percent lower is associated with intrafirm export prices that are 1.3% lower and intrafirm import prices that are .60% higher, relative to the tax effects for non-intrafirm goods.[21] This is consistent with tax minimization incentives. Other variables are similar to those in the previous specification: prices are higher when the price is inputed, when a link price is present, and when the transaction is not denominated in dollars.[22]

Table 8 shows regressions similar to those in Table 7. The only difference is that the intrafirm trade variables are now separated into the different types of intrafirm trade: market-based, cost-based, "other", and non-specified. Controlling for other variables, the intrafirm dummies indicate that these goods have higher prices than non-intrafirm goods, with the exception of "other" intrafirm trade.

Again, intrafirm prices also appear to be more sensitive to exchange rate differences. All of the coefficients on the exchange rate interaction terms are negative and statistically significant, again with the notable exception of "other". In terms of tax sensitivity, the results again indicate that intrafirm exports to low tax countries tend to have lower prices, and intrafirm imports from such countries tend to have higher prices, with only one exception ("other" intrafirm imports). The tax interaction coefficients are largest for cost-based intrafirm trade. For such goods, a tax rate one percent lower is

---

[21] The tables show elasticities with respect to (1-Effective Tax Rate). In the text, I discuss the implied elasticities with respect to the tax rate, which are calculated at the mean effective tax rate for the sample.

associated with intrafirm export prices that are 2.6% lower and intrafirm import prices that are 1.3% higher, again relative to the tax effects for non-intrafirm goods.[23] Other results are similar to those reported in Tables 6 and 7.

Table 9 turns to an analysis of the frequency of price changes observed in the data set. The probability of a monthly change in price is hypothesized to depend on whether the item is traded intrafirm, how much the exchange rate has changed in the last month and over the last six months, an interaction term that considers the effect of such changes in the exchange rate when trade is intrafirm, and dummy variables that indicate if a price is inputed during the months considered, if there is a link price present in the months considered, or if the price of the item in question is not denominated in dollars. It is expected that price changes will be more likely when trade is non-intrafirm, when exchange rate changes are larger, when there is an inputed price, when there is a link price, or when the price is not denominated in dollars. (If a good is denominated in foreign currency, the dollar price will automatically change even if the foreign currency price is constant since the exchange rate will typically change.)

Table 9 shows the results from probit regressions that estimate the probability of a monthly change in price. The coefficients that are reported indicate the change in the probability of the dependent variable (a change in price) given a change in the independent variable. Consider first the export equation. The intrafirm coefficient indicates that intrafirm exports are 8% less likely to experience a monthly change in price

---

[22] An alternative specification would be to include only those data that are not inputed in this analysis. This produces coefficients on the other variables that are quite similar to those found here.
[23] Again, note that the tables show elasticities with respect to (1-Effective Tax Rate). In the text, I discuss the implied elasticities with respect to the tax rate, which are calculated at the mean effective tax rate for the sample.

relative to non-intrafirm exports. A greater change in the exchange rate, either in the previous month, or in the previous six months, is associated with an increased probability of a change in price. For intrafirm exports, the interaction terms indicate that a change in price is even more likely given a change in the exchange rate. Goods with inputed prices are 26% more likely to experience changes in price. Goods where a link price is reported are also more likely to experience a price change, and goods reported in currencies other than the dollar are 59% more likely to see a monthly change in their (dollar) price.

For the import equation, most results are quite similar. The one important difference is that intrafirm imports are less likely to experience a monthly price change in response to changes in the exchange rate than non-intrafirm imports. The final column estimates imports and export together, and indicates that exports are less likely to see monthly price changes than are imports, controlling for changes in the other variables.

A Case Study

Most of the above results indicate that intrafirm trade appears to be more sensitive to exchange rates, with the exception of the import results for the above probit equations, where it appeared that import price changes were less likely in response to changes in exchange rates. In order to examine these relationships in a different light, I examined a case study of price changes for goods traded with Japan during this time period, 1997 to 1999.

Figure 3 shows the price movements for trade with Japan, as well as the yen/$ exchange rate during this period. Price indexes are created from the average monthly price changes for intrafirm and non-intrafirm trade. As shown, the yen/$ exchange rate exhibited substantial changes during this period. From June 1997 to August 1998, the

20

dollar experienced a substantial appreciation, from a value of 114 yen to a value of 144 yen. From August 1998 until December 1999, the dollar depreciated steadily, although not monotonically, from 144 yen to 102 yen.

Considering first Figure 3a, it appears that intrafirm trade responds with less magnitude to these exchange rate shifts. During the dollar appreciation, prices fell more sluggishly and did not fall as far; during the dollar depreciation, prices rose more slowly and did not increase as much. Examining figures 3b and 3c, one ascertains quickly that this pattern is more in evidence for imports than for exports. For imports, intrafirm prices clearly respond to a lesser degree to exchange rate changes than do non-intrafirm prices. For exports, however, no clear pattern emerges. During the initial dollar appreciation, intrafirm price changes are quite similar to non-intrafirm price changes. During the dollar depreciation, intrafirm prices appear to increase more rapidly than do non-intrafirm prices.

Implications for BLS Methodology

As discussed above, the BLS currently includes intrafirm trade prices in the construction of international trade price indexes by the IPP. While it is the current practice of the IPP to include all types of intrafirm trade prices, prior to 1998, only those intrafirm trade prices that were deemed to be market-based were included. The above analysis is instructive for considering how these practices are affecting trade price indexes.

Perhaps one should begin by stating that intrafirm trade should be included in international trade price indexes, if for no other reason than the fact that intrafirm trade accounts for a large fraction (currently about 40%) of all U.S. international trade. In addition, it appears from the above analysis that the price patterns of this trade are quite similar to those of non-intrafirm trade. In particular, year over year price changes are quite similar for both types of trade, regardless of whether one considers average price changes or the average absolute value of price changes. While intrafirm trade is somewhat less likely to experience monthly changes in price (41% of observations relative to 45% for non-intrafirm trade), the overall patterns of monthly price changes illustrated in figures one and two indicate that differences between the pricing behavior of intrafirm and non-intrafirm trade are neither large nor particularly systematic.

Nonetheless, the above generalizations are based on the entire sample of price observations. When one considers more narrowly trade in particular industries or with particular countries, larger differences may be evident. For instance, figure 3 illustrates that price patterns for intrafirm and non-intrafirm trade with Japan differed during this time period. Further, Table 3 indicates that there are some industries where price patterns may be more different for these two types of trade. Thus, when considering more detailed price indexes, it remains possible that intrafirm prices may experience different patterns.

Turning to the types of intrafirm trade, it is clear from the above analysis that "other, non-market based" intrafirm trade prices behave differently from the market-based or cost-based intrafirm trade prices. Monthly changes in prices are less likely, and the year over year price changes themselves are quite different. Further, in the regression analysis, prices for this type of intrafirm trade behaved atypically.

The prices of market, cost-based, and unclassified intrafirm trade also displayed differences from non-intrafirm trade. In particular, intrafirm trade prices were typically more correlated with exchange rate levels, and were also shown to be consistent with tax-minimizing behavior. Still, while these observations are interesting and important, and may be particularly important for some countries or industries, the percent of the variation in trade prices accounted for by these variables is quite small. In particular, if one considers regressions similar to those in Tables 7 or 8 that only include intrafirm variables (i.e., dummies and interaction terms), exchange rates, and tax rates, one finds that these variables account for only between one and five percent of the total variation in the dependent variable. In contrast, industry dummies and the other variables account for substantially more variation.[24]

My summary recommendations for the IPP are as follows.

- Continue to collect and utilize price data from intrafirm trade transactions.

- Continue to collect information on *whether* transactions are intrafirm. This will provide useful information for future study of these and other questions.

- Consider excluding those intrafirm prices where prices are neither market-based nor cost-based. (This accounts for only approximately one quarter of one percent of trade prices.)

- Particularly with respect to more detailed trade price indexes, be aware that intrafirm trade may behave differently from arms-length trade. This may be particularly important with respect to some stimuli, such as tax rate differences or exchange rate changes.

---

[24] Detailed results are available from the author upon request.

IV. Conclusions

This paper has analyzed data from the BLS on international prices between 1997 and 1999 in order to investigate the behavior of intrafirm trade prices. This research has illuminated several important ways in which intrafirm trade prices differ from arms-length prices. In addition, there are implications for the construction of international price indexes by the BLS.

First, intrafirm trade appears to be influenced by the tax-minimization strategies of multinational firms. In particular, there is a strong and statistically significant relationship between a country's tax rate and the prices of intrafirm imports and exports transacted with that country. The estimates in Table 7 indicate that a tax rate one percent lower is associated with intrafirm export prices that are 1.3% lower and intrafirm import prices that are .60% higher, relative to non-intrafirm goods. As Table 8 indicates, these tax effects are strongest for the intrafirm trade which is cost-based. For such goods, a tax rate one percent lower is associated with intrafirm export prices that are 2.6% lower and intrafirm import prices that are 1.3% higher, again relative to non-intrafirm goods.

Second, intrafirm trade prices are more correlated with exchange rate index levels than are non-intrafirm trade prices. In particular, a stronger dollar is associated with lower export and import prices, but particularly so for intrafirm exports and imports. The estimates in Table 7 indicate that a 1% stronger exchange rate index (indicating a stronger dollar) is associated with export prices that are .6% lower in general, but 1.6% lower for intrafirm goods. Similarly, a 1% stronger dollar is associated with import prices that are .4% lower in general, but .7% lower for intrafirm goods. Still, all evidence

24

does not indicate that intrafirm goods are more responsive to exchange rate changes. When one considers the probability of a change in price, one finds that intrafirm export prices are more likely to change in response to changes in exchange rates than are non-intrafirm export prices. Still, the opposite is true for import prices, where intrafirm import prices are less likely to change in response to changes in exchange rates. This same pattern is also in evidence when one considers a case study of price changes for trade with Japan during 1997-1999, a period where the dollar first appreciated strongly, and then depreciated, vis a vis the yen.

Still, when one examines the extent of variation in trade prices that is explained by these variables (intrafirm dummies or interaction terms, exchange rates, and tax rates), one finds that the overall explanatory power of these variables is relatively low. Further, the overall price patterns for intrafirm trade are not very different from those for non-intrafirm trade. The average magnitudes of price changes are comparable, and the patterns of such changes over time are also similar. Therefore, one should not overemphasize the differences between intrafirm trade and non-intrafirm trade. While there may be important differences at a detailed level, or with respect to some stimuli, the overall behavior of intrafirm trade prices is quite similar to that of non-intrafirm trade prices.

Therefore, the IPP should certainly continue to sample prices from intrafirm trade transactions, and to include such prices in the subsequent construction of price indexes. The one exception to be considered would be "other, non-market based" trade, where prices appear to be substantially out of line with those of other goods.

References

Alterman, William. 1997a. "Are producer prices good proxies for export prices?" *Monthly Labor Review*. October. 18-32.

Alterman, William. 1997b. "A Comparison of the Export and Producer Price Indexes for Semiconductors." Photocopy. July.

Buijink, Willem, et al. 1999. "Final Report of a Study on Corporate Effective Tax Rates in the European Union." April. photocopy.

Bureau of Economic Analysis. *U.S. Direct Investment Abroad: Operations of U.S. Parent Companies and Their Foreign Affiliates*. 1997.

Bureau of Labor Statistics. 1999. *International Trade Price Indexes and Seasonal Commodities*. Washington: U.S. Department of Labor.

Caves, Richard E. 1996. *Multinational Enterprise and Economic Analysis*. 2nd edition. New York: Cambridge U P.

Clausing, Kimberly A. 1998. "The Impact of Transfer Pricing on Intrafirm Trade." *NBER Working Paper no.6688* , forthcoming within U of Chicago Press volume.

Clausing, Kimberly A. 2000. "The Empirical Behavior of Intrafirm Trade in a Gravity Equation Model." Draft. March.

Eden, Lorraine. 1998. *Taxing Multinationals: Transfer Pricing and Corporate Income Taxation in North America*. Toronto: U of Toronto Press.

Encarnation, Dennis. 1992. *Rivals Beyond Trade: American versus Japan in Global Competition*. Ithaca: Cornell U Press.

Goldsbrough, David J. 1981. "International Trade of Multinational Corporations and Its Responsiveness to Changes in Aggregate Demand and Relative Prices." *International Monetary Fund Staff Papers*. 28(3). 573-99.

Horst, Thomas. 1971. The Theory of the Multinational Firm: Optimal Behavior Under Different Tariff and Tax Rates." *Journal of Political Economy*. 79(5). 1059-72.

Kant, Chander. 1995. "Minority Ownership, Deferral, Perverse Intrafirm Trade and Tariffs." *International Economic Journal*. 9(1). 19-37.

Kant, Chander. 1990. "Multinational Firms and Government Revenue." *Journal of Public Economics*. 42(2). 135-147.

Knetter, Michael M. 1993. "International Comparisons of Pricing-to-Market Behavior." *American Economic Review*. 83(3). 473-86.

Lipsey, Robert E. and Kravis, Irving B. 1986. "The Competitiveness and Comparative Advantage of U.S. Multinationals, 1957-1983." *National Bureau of Economic Research Working Paper no. 3051*. October.

Little, Jane Sneddon. 1986. "Intra-firm Trade and U.S. Protectionism: Thoughts Based on a Small Survey." *New England Economic Review*. Jan/Feb. 46-51.

Rangan, Subramanian, and Robert Z. Lawrence. 1999. *A Prism on Globalization: Corporate Responses to the Dollar*. Washington: Brookings Institution Press.

Rauch, James E. 1996. "Networks versus Markets in International Trade." *NBER Working Paper no. 5617*. June.

Zeile, William J. 1997. "U.S. Intrafirm Trade in Goods." *Survey of Current Business*. February. 23-38.

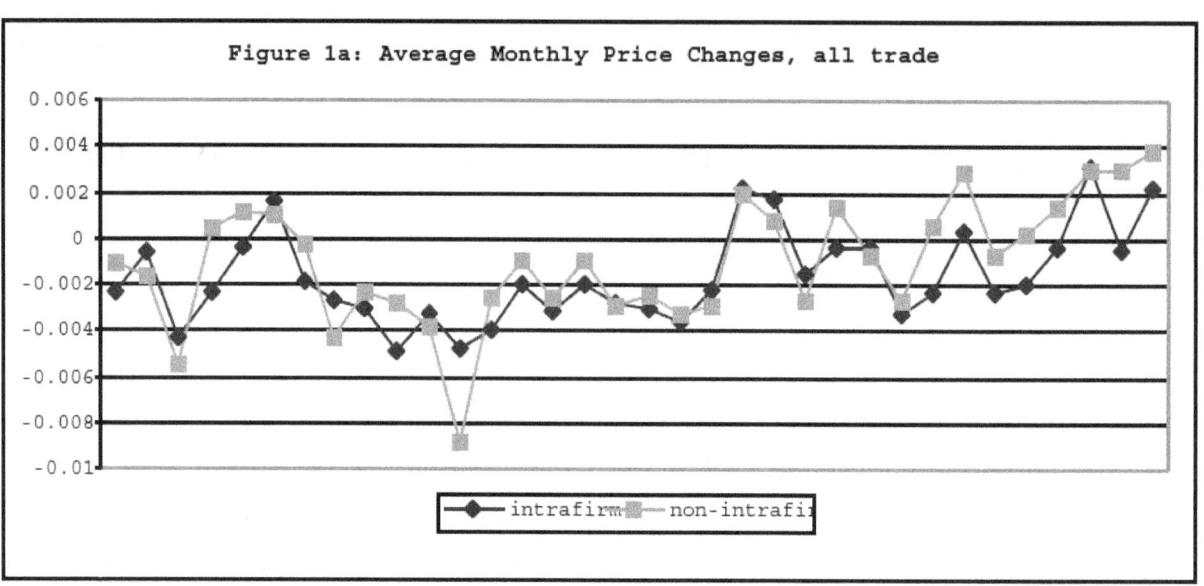

Figure 1a: Average Monthly Price Changes, all trade

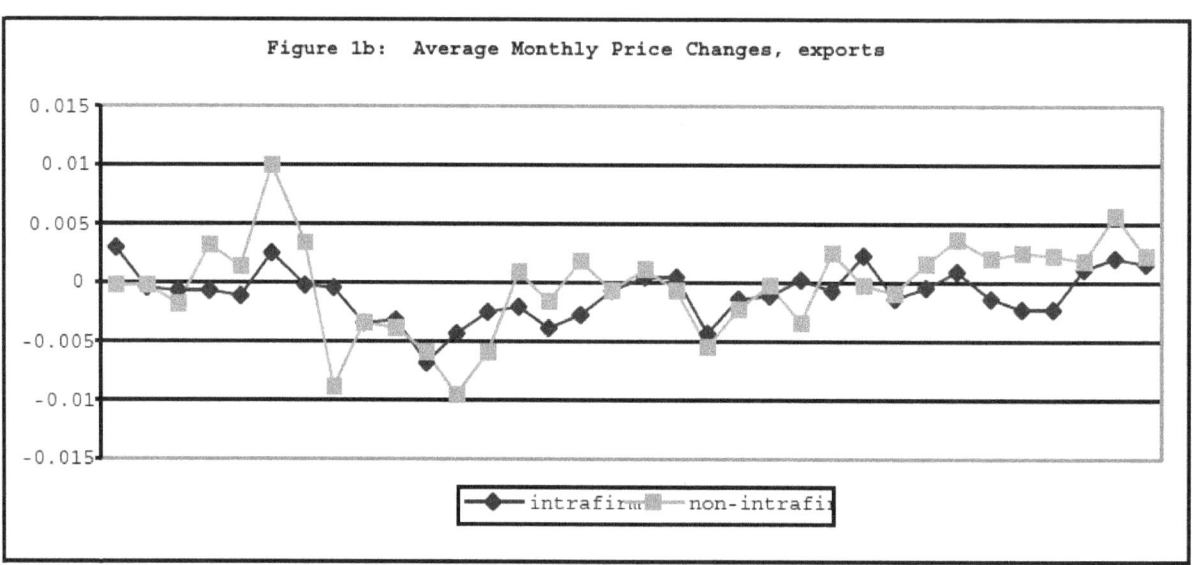

Figure 1b: Average Monthly Price Changes, exports

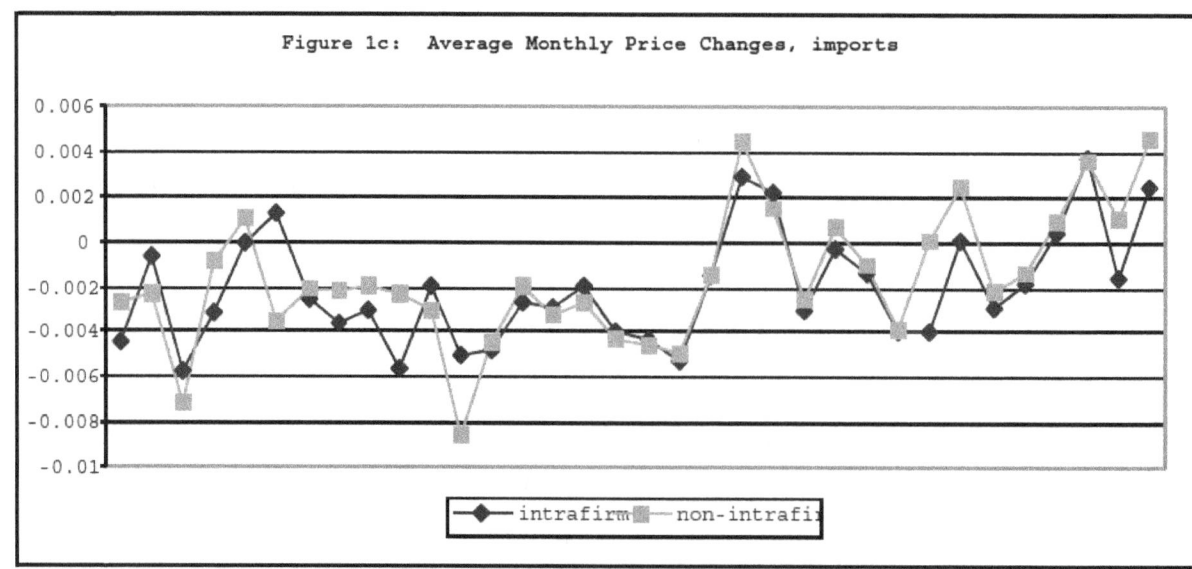

Figure 1c: Average Monthly Price Changes, imports

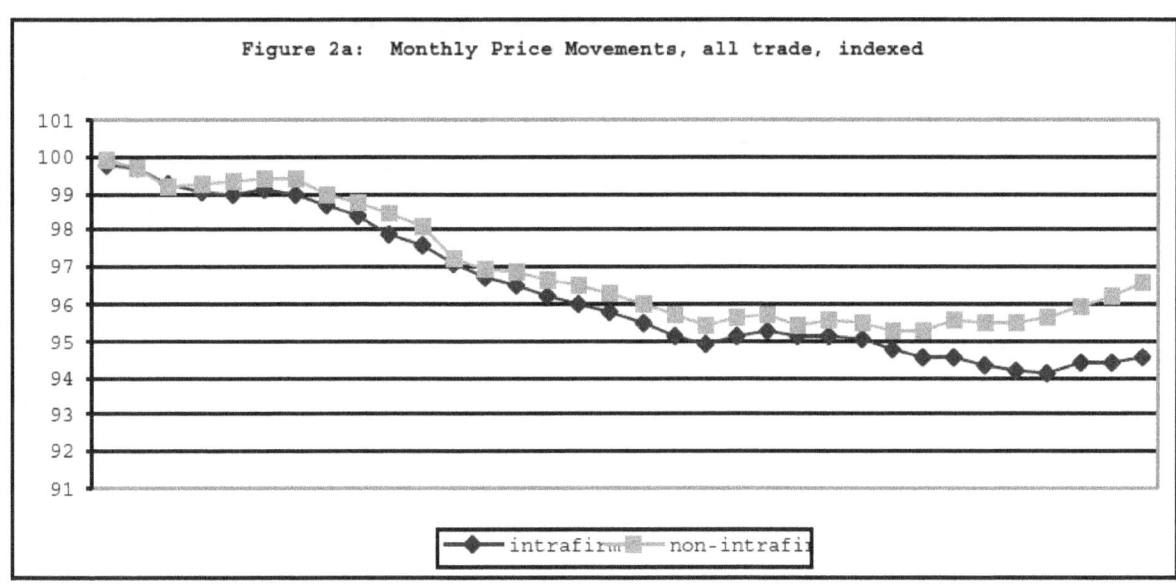

Figure 2a: Monthly Price Movements, all trade, indexed

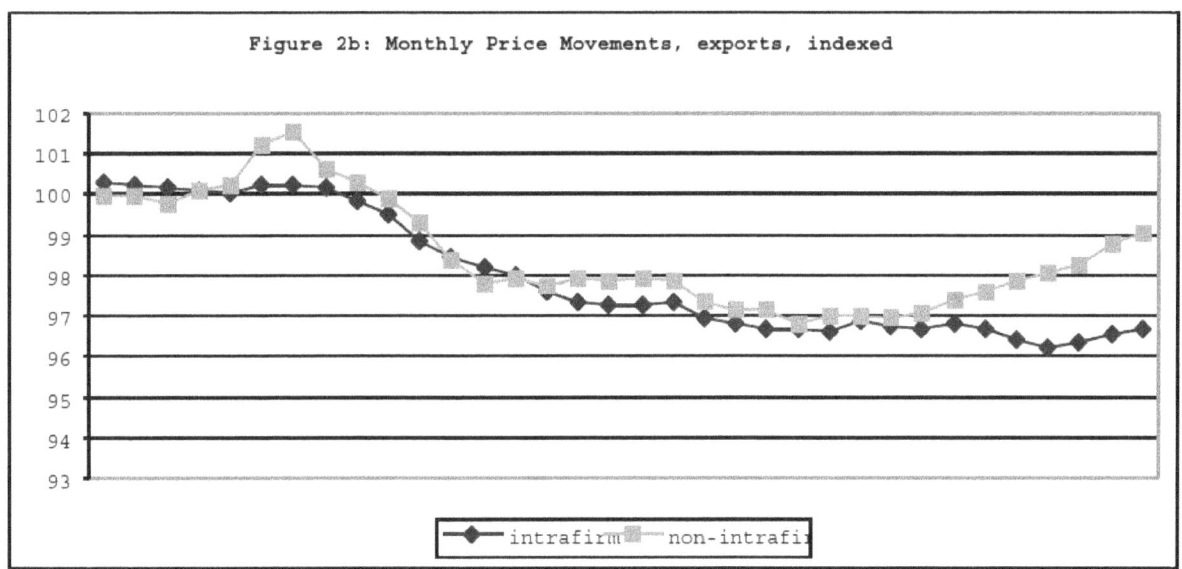

Figure 2b: Monthly Price Movements, exports, indexed

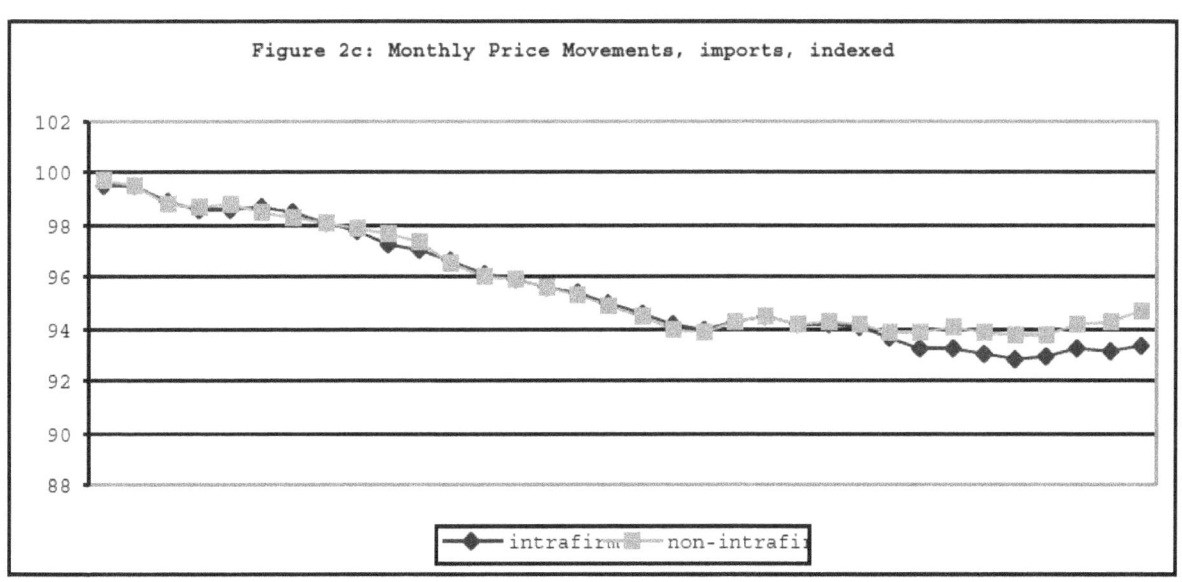

Figure 2c: Monthly Price Movements, imports, indexed

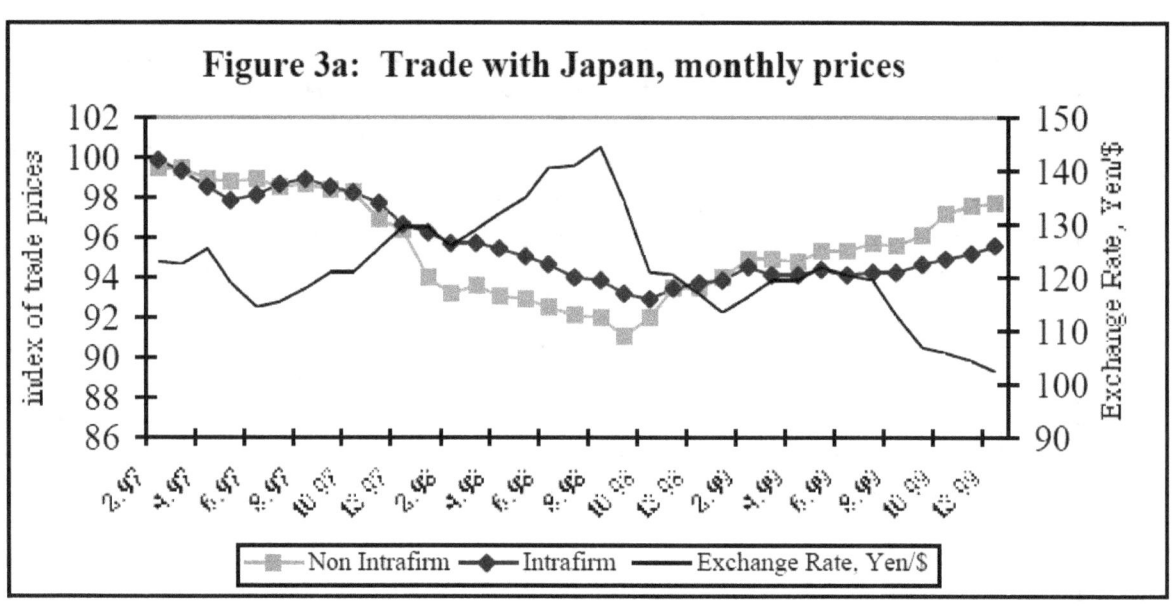

Figure 3a: Trade with Japan, monthly prices

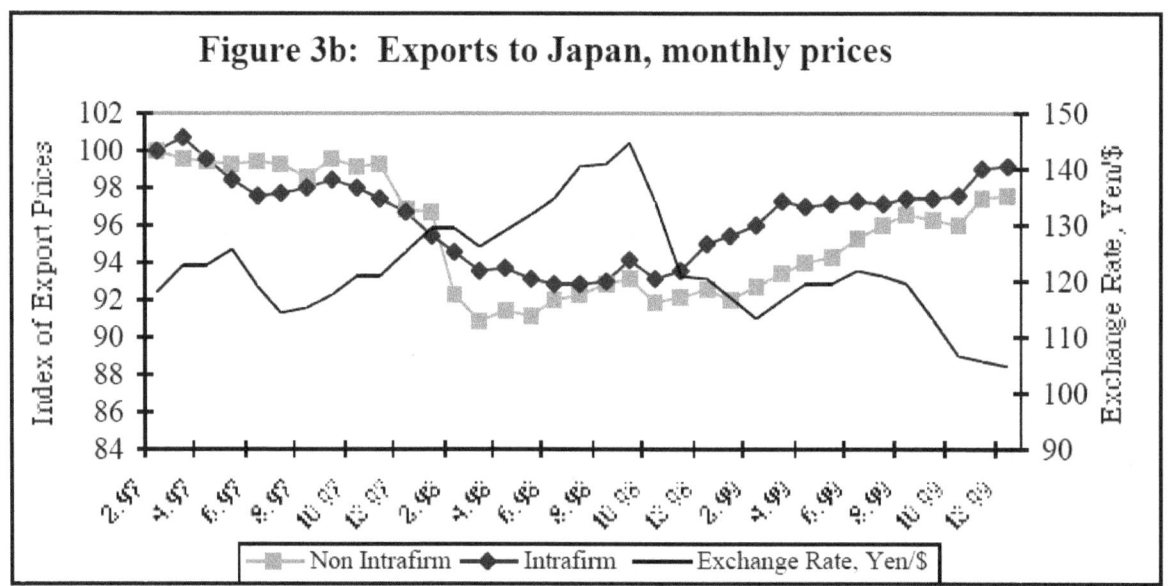

Figure 3b: Exports to Japan, monthly prices

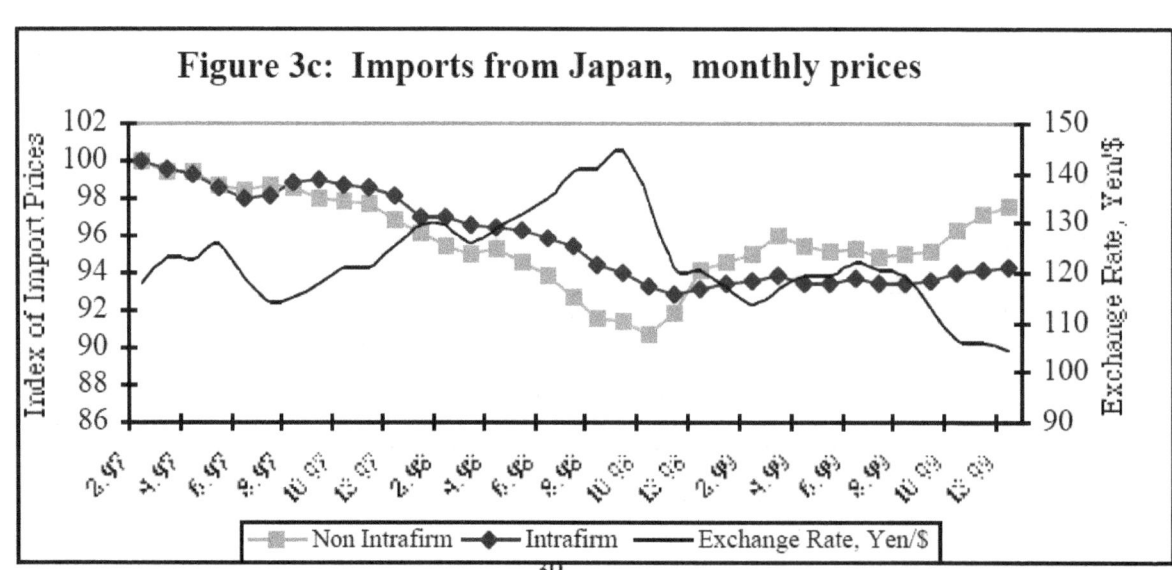

Figure 3c: Imports from Japan, monthly prices

Table 1: Descriptive Statistics

Number of Monthly Observations	426,670			
% of Observations that are Exports	33.1			
% of Observations that are Intrafirm Transactions	38.2			
Of which:	Market-Based	Cost-Based	"Other"	Not Classified
	11.1%	5.6%	0.7%	82.6%
% Of Observations that are Inputed	42.0			
% Of Observations where a link price is available	0.3			
Mean Effective Tax Rate for Observations in the Sample *	32.1% (Standard Deviation = 14.2)			

*This variable is defined and discussed on p.14 of the text.

Table 2:   Price Changes for Intrafirm and Non-intrafirm Trade

	Intrafirm	Non Intrafirm
All Trade		
% Change in Price, Year over Year, sample average	-1.3	-1.1
Absolute Value of % Change in Price, Year over Year, sample average	7.4	7.5
% of Observations with a Change in Observed Price, month to month	40.8	45.1
Exports		
% Change in Price, Year over Year, sample average	-0.2	-0.6
Absolute Value of % Change in Price, Year over Year, sample average	8.0	6.9
% of Observations with a Change in Observed Price, month to month	36.9	40.3
Imports		
% Change in Price, Year over Year, sample average	-1.7	-1.4
Absolute Value of % Change in Price, Year over Year, Sample average	7.2	7.8
% of Observations with a Change in Observed Price, month to month	42.3	47.7

These figures indicate the average values for intrafirm and non-intrafirm trade, over the entire sample. Data are from the Bureau of Labor Statistics.

Table 3: Price Changes for Intrafirm and Non-Intrafirm Trade, by SITC industry

Imports

SITC 2 digit industry	Change in Price, year/year		Absolute Change in Price, year/year		Observations with a Monthly Change in Price	
	Intrafirm	Non-Intrafirm	Intrafirm	Non-Intrafirm	Intrafirm	Non-Intrafirm
03	1%	0%	14%	14%	74%	77%
05	-6%	-1%	15%	19%	56%	70%
11	1%	2%	1%	4%	34%	31%
23	-3%	-17%	4%	18%	81%	82%
24	10%	10%	13%	13%	60%	78%
27	-3%	-2%	6%	3%	30%	31%
42	0%	5%	9%	11%	89%	74%
51	-3%	-2%	10%	11%	48%	44%
52	-4%	-5%	13%	9%	39%	43%
54	-2%	3%	9%	7%	46%	50%
55	-3%	-3%	8%	6%	64%	41%
57	5%	2%	12%	7%	40%	45%
58	-8%	-2%	16%	6%	51%	49%
59	-7%	-4%	13%	8%	33%	24%
62	0%	-1%	4%	3%	34%	30%
64	-3%	-5%	7%	8%	61%	48%
65	-1%	-3%	3%	5%	40%	49%
66	0%	0%	4%	4%	49%	33%
67	-5%	-8%	8%	10%	55%	58%
68	1%	1%	10%	14%	58%	84%
69	-3%	-1%	8%	7%	43%	52%
71	-1%	0%	5%	5%	32%	40%
72	0%	2%	5%	6%	47%	45%
73	-1%	0%	4%	4%	37%	45%
74	1%	-1%	7%	7%	39%	42%
75	-6%	-8%	11%	12%	46%	54%
76	-2%	-4%	5%	6%	29%	38%
77	-3%	-2%	8%	9%	42%	48%
78	1%	2%	5%	6%	35%	42%
79	3%	1%	8%	3%	21%	24%
81	-7%	0%	8%	4%	49%	38%
82	-11%	-3%	12%	4%	31%	46%
83	5%	1%	7%	5%	36%	44%
84	0%	-1%	5%	4%	38%	35%
85	-1%	-1%	3%	3%	65%	44%
87	-1%	-1%	5%	5%	37%	38%
88	0%	0%	5%	4%	41%	41%
89	-2%	-1%	5%	5%	40%	41%

Table 3: Price Changes for Intrafirm and Non-Intrafirm Trade, by SITC industry (Continued)

Exports

SITC 2 digit industry	Change in Price, year/year		Absolute Change in Price, year/year		Observations with a Monthly Change in Price	
	Intrafirm	Non-Intrafirm	Intrafirm	Non-Intrafirm	Intrafirm	Non-Intrafirm
01	15%	0%	23%	18%	85%	85%
03	14%	12%	26%	22%	78%	74%
04	-2%	-5%	7%	9%	55%	42%
05	8%	3%	12%	23%	39%	69%
11	-4%	1%	4%	8%	35%	27%
23	-9%	-5%	10%	6%	45%	42%
24	1%	1%	9%	10%	59%	63%
51	-2%	-3%	9%	10%	36%	43%
52	2%	-1%	8%	4%	31%	28%
54	-2%	-3%	8%	9%	15%	18%
55	2%	2%	5%	4%	26%	29%
57	-1%	-1%	5%	10%	35%	47%
58	-2%	0%	4%	4%	36%	48%
59	-2%	-1%	7%	8%	33%	29%
62	19%	-3%	23%	7%	77%	28%
64	-2%	0%	11%	7%	53%	47%
66	-3%	0%	9%	2%	27%	25%
67	-2%	-7%	4%	7%	30%	42%
68	1%	-1%	6%	12%	78%	78%
69	0%	0%	5%	6%	38%	37%
71	1%	1%	4%	4%	25%	18%
72	-2%	1%	7%	2%	41%	28%
74	0%	1%	3%	4%	25%	26%
75	-8%	-3%	12%	6%	46%	47%
76	-2%	-2%	7%	4%	29%	29%
77	-1%	-2%	7%	8%	37%	37%
78	1%	0%	3%	2%	31%	35%
79	-2%	-2%	8%	4%	37%	26%
84	-9%	-4%	14%	9%	37%	26%
87	2%	1%	7%	3%	41%	27%
89	-1%	0%	7%	3%	30%	41%

(Note: These tables include only those industries with more than 100 observations for all of the variables. Complete tables of all industries are available upon request. However, comparisons of price patterns for the other industries are particularly difficult.)

Table 4: Share of Observations that are Intrafirm by SITC Industry

SITC	Intra-Firm	Market	Cost	Other	n.a.	SITC	Intra-Firm	Market	Cost	Other	n.a.
All	38%	4%	2%	0.3%	32%	55	38%	2%	1%	0%	36%
00	30%	0%	0%	0%	30%	56	26%	1%	3%	0%	23%
01	20%	8%	1%	0%	10%	57	42%	2%	2%	0%	39%
02	37%	2%	0%	0%	36%	58	39%	2%	1%	0%	36%
03	19%	2%	0%	0%	17%	59	62%	6%	3%	0%	53%
04	20%	1%	9%	0%	11%	61	16%	1%	6%	0%	10%
05	18%	4%	4%	0%	11%	62	52%	2%	1%	0%	49%
06	39%	1%	3%	0%	35%	63	14%	2%	0%	0%	11%
07	18%	3%	2%	0%	14%	64	28%	5%	1%	0%	21%
08	18%	5%	6%	0%	8%	65	19%	3%	3%	0%	13%
09	70%	7%	9%	0%	54%	66	25%	5%	2%	0%	19%
11	17%	3%	1%	0%	14%	67	41%	7%	1%	0%	33%
12	19%	1%	0%	1%	17%	68	33%	6%	0%	0%	27%
21	33%	2%	0%	0%	32%	69	28%	4%	3%	0%	21%
*22	43%	0%	19%	0%	24%	71	41%	3%	3%	0%	35%
23	28%	1%	0%	1%	27%	72	50%	4%	3%	0%	44%
24	39%	2%	1%	0%	37%	73	51%	4%	1%	0%	47%
25	8%	2%	0%	1%	5%	74	39%	3%	1%	1%	34%
26	5%	2%	2%	0%	1%	75	58%	6%	3%	0%	50%
27	47%	10%	0%	0%	37%	76	52%	2%	1%	0%	49%
28	17%	5%	4%	0%	9%	77	50%	4%	2%	0%	43%
29	23%	6%	8%	0%	10%	78	41%	7%	4%	1%	30%
32	2%	0%	0%	0%	2%	79	54%	6%	11%	4%	34%
33	11%	0%	0%	0%	11%	81	24%	4%	0%	0%	20%
34	6%	0%	0%	0%	6%	82	21%	3%	2%	0%	16%
41	0%	0%	0%	0%	0%	83	26%	3%	0%	0%	23%
42	61%	27%	2%	0%	31%	84	16%	1%	2%	0%	13%
*43	88%	0%	0%	0%	88%	85	11%	2%	0%	0%	9%
51	39%	3%	1%	0%	34%	87	59%	7%	3%	1%	49%
52	44%	2%	0%	0%	42%	88	59%	12%	2%	0%	46%
53	61%	1%	8%	0%	52%	89	28%	5%	2%	0%	21%
54	65%	7%	3%	0%	56%	*97	58%	22%	0%	0%	36%

35

Table 5: Price Patterns by Type of Trade

	Market Based	Cost Based	Other	Intrafirm Not Classified	Non-Intrafirm Trade
All Trade					
% Change in Price, Year over Year, sample average	0.4	0.4	-11.4	-1.4	-1.1
Absolute Value of % Change in Price, Year over Year, sample average	8.1	8.6	13.3	7.3	7.5
% of Observations with a Change in Observed Price, month to month	41.2	37.2	28.7	41.0	45.1
Exports					
% Change in Price, Year over Year, sample average	1.2	0.8	-3.5	-0.4	-0.6
Absolute Value of % Change in Price, Year over Year, sample average	11.9	9.5	6.9	7.7	6.9
% of Observations with a Change in Observed Price, month to month	40.1	36.3	25.5	36.7	40.3
Imports					
% Change in Price, Year over Year, sample average	0.1	-0.2	-13.5	-1.9	-1.4
Absolute Value of % Change in Price, Year over Year, sample average	6.8	7.6	15.0	7.2	7.8
% of Observations with a Change in Observed Price, month to month	41.7	38.0	30.5	42.7	47.7

This table shows the average value of the price variables for different categories of intrafirm trade (market-based, cost-based, other, and not classified) as well as for non-intrafirm trade.

Table 6: Price Regressions, Separating Intrafirm and Non-Intrafirm Trade

Independent Variables	*Exports* Intrafirm	Non-Intrafirm	*Imports* Intrafirm	Non-Intrafirm
Exchange Rate	-1.544 (.1114)	-.5583 (.0593)	-.7303 (.0596)	-.4035 (.0263)
1- Effective Tax Rate	-3.196 (.1218)	-.5086 (.0801)	-.7990 (.0655)	-1.971 (.0394)
Inpute	.1202 (.0267)	.1723 (.0192)	-.0279 (.0180)	.0356 (.0118)
Link	.6859 (.1757)	.6046 (.1607)	.3604 (.1510)	.2924 (.1128)
No Dollar	.4821 (.0622)	.0683 (.0628)	.0514 (.0301)	.2815 (.0208)
Industry Dummies	Yes	Yes	Yes	Yes
# of obs.	44,646	90,575	113,711	162,175
Adjusted R^2	.410	.399	.316	.379
F	470.3	863.5	835.4	1522.6
Prob > F	0.000	0.000	0.000	0.000

Note: All variables except dummy variables are in natural logs. Standard errors are in parentheses.

Table 7: Price Regressions,
Intrafirm and Non-Intrafirm Trade Estimated Together

Independent Variables	Exports	Imports
Intrafirm Dummy	3.494 (.6140)	2.576 (.2821)
Exchange Rate	-.6170 (.0590)	-.4216 (.0293)
1- Effective Tax Rate	-.5201 (.0792)	-2.080 (.0440)
Intrafirm Dummy *Exchange Rate	-1.020 (.1275)	-.3446 (.0600)
Intrafirm Dummy *(1-Effective Tax Rate)	-2.737 (.1402)	1.261 (.0717)
Inpute	.1579 (.0156)	.0190 (.0102)
Link	.6286 (.1206)	.3534 (.0925)
No Dollar	.3364 (.0442)	.1759 (.0175)
Industry Dummies	Yes	Yes
# of obs.	135,221	275,886
Adjusted R^2	.381	.353
F	1188	2185
Prob > F	0.000	0.000

Note: All variables except dummy variables are in natural logs. Standard errors are in parentheses.

**Table 8: Price Regressions,
Including Different Types of Intrafirm Trade**

Independent Variables	Exports	Imports
Market Intrafirm Dummy	9.453 (1.653)	3.069 (.6240)
Cost Intrafirm Dummy	3.174 (1.932)	11.85 (1.121)
"Other" Intrafirm Dummy	-17.44 (10.15)	-1.035 (2.777)
Non-spec. Intrafirm Dummy	2.427 (.6733)	1.971 (.3121)
Exchange Rate	-.6167 (.0590)	-.4202 (.0293)
1- Effective Tax Rate	-.5175 (.0792)	-2.077 (.0440)
Mkt. Intrafirm Dummy *Exchange Rate	-2.065 (.3407)	-.3807 (.1302)
Cost Intrafirm Dummy *Exchange Rate	-1.153 (.3935)	-2.247 (.2326)
"Other" Intrafirm Dummy *Exchange Rate	3.400 (2.133)	-.0967 (.5728)
Non-spec. Intrafirm Dummy *Exchange Rate	-0.800 (.1401)	-.2232 (.0652)
Mkt.Intrafirm Dummy *(1-Effective Tax Rate)	-.4611 (.3573)	1.411 (.1613)
Cost Intrafirm Dummy *(1-Effective Tax Rate)	-5.423 (.4446)	2.719 (.2999)
Other Intrafirm Dummy *(1-Effective Tax Rate)	-2.135 (1.201)	-6.425 (.7869)
N-sp. Intrafirm Dummy *(1-Effective Tax Rate)	-2.752 (.1515)	.2232 (.0652)
Inpute	.1629 (.0156)	.0209 (.0102)
Link	.6197 (.1205)	.3448 (.0925)
No Dollar	.3437 (.0442)	.1789 (.0175)
Industry Dummies	Yes	Yes
# of obs.	135,221	275,886
Adjusted R^2	.381	.354
F	1056	1940
Prob > F	0.000	0.000

Note: All variables except dummy variables are in natural logs. Standard errors are in parentheses.

Table 9: Probit Regressions
Estimating the Probability of a Monthly Change in Price

Independent Variables	Exports	Imports	All Trade
Intrafirm Dummy	-.0886	-.0608	-.0673
	(.0047)	(.0033)	(.0027)
Absolute Value of Change in Exchange Rate, last month	.1978	.4313	.3448
	(.0896)	(.0667)	(.0531)
Absolute Value of Change in Exchange Rate, last 6 months	.1086	.2234	.1915
	(.0296)	(.0196)	(.0162)
Intrafirm Dummy *Exchange Rate Variable	.2880	-.4212	-.3203
	(.1525)	(.0699)	(.0576)
Intrafirm Dummy *6 month Exchange Rate Variable	.2666	-.3185	-.1391
	(.0546)	(.0340)	(.0279)
Inpute	.2610	.2811	.2753
	(.0031)	(.0024)	(.0019)
Link	.2713	.2823	.2798
	(.0217)	(.0160)	(.0129)
No Dollar	.5872	.5678	.5751
	(.0054)	(.0024)	(.0022)
Export			-.0414
			(.0021)
# of obs.	86,317	173,792	260,109
Psuedo R^2	.094	.140	.127
χ^2	10,410	32,829	44,170
Prob > χ^2	0.000	0.000	0.000

Note: Coefficients reported are the change in the probability of the dependent variable (a change in price) given a change in the independent variables, or dF/dx where F is the probability function and x is the independent variable. However, for the dummy variables, dF/dx is for a discrete change of the dummy variable from 0 to 1. Standard errors are in parentheses.